To Beth,

Happy Anniversary

From Your Secret Sis,

Joann Lambert

Poems of Love

Poems of Love

Edited by Gail Harvey

AVENEL BOOKS
New York

To A. H.
With Love

Compilation and introduction copyright © 1989 by
Outlet Book Company, Inc.
All rights reserved.
First published in 1989 by Avenel Books, distributed by
Outlet Book Company, Inc., a Random House Company,
225 Park Avenue South, New York, New York 10003.
Manufactured in Singapore

Designed by Don Bender

Library of Congress Cataloging-in-Publication Data

Poems of love / edited by Gail Harvey.
        p.   cm.
    ISBN 0-517-69200-7
    1. Love poetry, English.   2. Love poetry, American.
I. Harvey, Gail.
PR1184.P63   1989
821.008'0354—dc20
                                        89-34411
                                        CIP

12   11   10   9   8   7   6   5

Contents

Introduction

I love you. These three small words have inspired poets since the beginning of time. Love has many facets and the world's great poets have written of love faithful and faithless, love old and new, of love's lust and longing, power and regret, torments and pain. And, of course, many have sung the praises of their own beloveds.

Poems of Love is a collection of memorable poems from different times and many places, all written, unquestionably, from the heart and covering many aspects of what is surely the strongest of human emotions. In *Upon the Sand*, for example, Ella Wheeler Wilcox writes of the need for love to have "friendship for its base." George, Lord Lyttelton asks his heart "if this be love?" In *April Love*, Ernest Dowson immortalizes a love "as free as the wind on the hill." William Wordsworth describes his beloved as "a phantom of delight . . . a perfect woman . . . with something of an angel-light" and Edmund Waller compares the woman he adores to a lovely rose. Anne Bradstreet writes a moving tribute to her husband

and in *The Poet's Song to His Wife* Barry Cornwall asks, "How many summers, love, have I been thine?"

Included, too, are wonderful love sonnets by William Shakespeare and Elizabeth Barrett Browning, as well as Christopher Marlowe's delightful poem *The Shepherd to His Love* and Edgar Allan Poe's plaintive *Annabel Lee*.

Poems of Love is a celebration of love in all its guises. Some of these poems express tenderness, others passion. Some are flowery and many are subtle. This is a collection that is sure to touch and delight anyone who has ever been in love.

GAIL HARVEY

NEW YORK
1989

I WILL TELL THEE
WHAT IT IS TO LOVE

Love? I will tell thee what it is to love!
It is to build with human thoughts a shrine,
Where Hope sits brooding like a beauteous dove;
Where Time seems young, and Life a thing divine.
All tastes, all pleasures, all desires combine
To consecrate this sanctuary of bliss.
Above, the stars in cloudless beauty shine;
Around, the streams their flowery margins kiss;
And if there's heaven on earth, that heaven is surely this.

Yes, this is Love, the steadfast and the true,
The immortal glory which hath never set;
The best, the brightest boon the heart e'er knew:
Of all life's sweets the very sweetest yet!
O' who but can recall the eve they met
To breathe, in some green walk, their first young vow?
While summer flowers with moonlight dews were wet,
And winds sighed soft around the mountain's brow,
And all was rapture then which is but memory now!

CHARLES SWAIN

ANSWER TO A CHILD'S QUESTION

Do you ask what the birds say? The sparrow,
    the dove,
The linnet, and thrush say "I love, and I love!"
In the winter they're silent, the wind is so strong;
What it says I don't know, but it sings a loud
    song.
But green leaves, and blossoms, and sunny
    warm weather,
And singing and loving—all come back together.
But the lark is so brimful of gladness and love,
The green fields below him, the blue sky above,
That he sings, and he sings, and forever sings he,
"I love my Love, and my Love loves me."

SAMUEL COLERIDGE

UPON THE SAND

All love that has not friendship for its base,
  Is like a mansion built upon the sand.
Though brave its walls as any in the land,
And its tall turrets lift their heads in grace;
Though skillful and accomplished artists trace
  Most beautiful designs on every hand,
  And gleaming statues in dim niches stand,
And fountains play in some flow'r-hidden place:

Yet, when from the frowning east a sudden gust
  Of adverse fate is blown, or sad rains fall
  Day in, day out, against its yielding wall,
Lo! the fair structure crumbles to the dust.
Love, to endure life's sorrow and earth's woe,
Needs friendship's solid masonwork below.

ELLA WHEELER WILCOX

}11{

TELL ME, MY HEART, IF THIS
BE LOVE

When Delia on the plain appears,
Awed by a thousand tender fears,
I would approach, but dare not move;—
Tell me, my heart, if this be love.

Whene'er she speaks, my ravished ear
No other voice than hers can hear;
No other wit but hers approve;—
Tell me, my heart, if this be love.

If she some other swain commend,
Though I was once his fondest friend,
His instant enemy I prove;—
Tell me, my heart, if this be love.

When she is absent, I no more
Delight in all that pleased before,
The clearest spring, the shadiest grove;—
Tell me, my heart, if this be love.

When fond of power, of beauty vain,
Her nets she spread for every swain,
I strove to hate, but vainly strove;—
Tell me, my heart, if this be love.

GEORGE LYTTELTON

SHE WALKS IN BEAUTY

She walks in beauty, like the night
   Of cloudless climes and starry skies,
And all that's best of dark and bright
   Meets in her aspect and her eyes,
Thus mellowed to that tender light
   Which heaven to gaudy day denies.

One shade the more, one ray the less
   Had half impaired the nameless grace
Which waves in every raven tress
   Or softly lightens o'er her face,
Where thoughts serenely sweet express
   How pure, how dear their dwelling-place.

And on that cheek and o'er that brow
   So soft, so calm, yet eloquent,
The smiles that win, the tints that glow,
   But tell of days in goodness spent,—
A mind at peace with all below,
   A heart whose love is innocent.

GEORGE GORDON, LORD BYRON

AH! WHAT IS LOVE?

*A*h! What is love? It is a pretty thing,
As sweet unto a shepherd as a king,
    And sweeter too;
For kings have cares that wait upon a crown,
And cares can make the sweetest face to frown:
    Ah then, ah then,
If country loves such sweet desires gain,
What lady would not love a shepherd swain?

His flocks are folded; he comes home at night
As merry as a king in his delight,
    And merrier too;
For kings bethink them what the state require,
Where shepherds, careless, carol by the fire:
    Ah then, ah then,
If country love such sweet desires gain,
What lady would not love a shepherd swain?

He kisseth first, then sits as blithe to eat
His cream and curd as doth the king his meat,
    And blither too;
For kings have often fears when they sup,
Where shepherds dread no poison in their cup:
    Ah then, ah then,
If country loves such sweet desires gain,
What lady would not love a shepherd swain?

Upon his couch of straw he sleeps as sound
As doth the king upon his beds of down,
    More sounder too;
For cares cause kings full oft their sleep to spill,
Where weary shepherds lie and snort their fill:
    Ah then, ah then,
If country loves such sweet desires gain,
What lady would not love a shepherd swain?

Thus with his wife he spends the year as blithe
As doth the king at every tide or syth,
    And blither too;
For kings have wars and broils to take in hand,
When shepherds laugh, and love upon the land:
    Ah then, ah then,
If country loves such sweet desires gain,
What lady would not love a shepherd swain?

ROBERT GREENE

A WOMAN'S QUESTION

$\mathcal{B}$efore I trust my fate to thee,
  Or place my hand in thine,
Before I let thy future give
  Color and form to mine,
Before I peril all for thee,
Question thy soul tonight for me.

I break all slighter bonds, nor feel
  A shadow of regret:
Is there one link within the past
  That holds thy spirit yet?
Or is thy faith as clear and free
As that which I can pledge to thee?

Does there within thy dimmest dreams
  A possible future shine,
Wherein thy life could henceforth breathe,
  Untouched, unshared by mine?
If so, at any pain or cost,
O, tell me before all is lost!

Look deeper still: if thou canst feel,
  Within thy inmost soul,
That thou hast kept a portion back,
  While I have staked the whole,
Let no false pity spare the blow,
But in true mercy tell me so.

Is there within thy heart a need
    That mine cannot fulfil?
One chord that any other hand
    Could better wake or still?
Speak now, lest at some future day
My whole life wither and decay.

Lives there within thy nature hid
    The demon-spirit, change,
Shedding a passing glory still
    On all things new and strange?
It may not be thy fault alone,—
But shield my heart against thine own.

Couldst thou withdraw thy hand one day
    And answer to my claim,
That fate, and that to-day's mistake,—
    Not thou,—had been to blame?
Some soothe their conscience thus; but thou
Wilt surely warn and save me now.

Nay, answer *not*,—I dare not hear,
    The words would come too late;
Yet I would spare thee all remorse,
    So comfort thee, my fate:
Whatever on my heart may fall,
Remember, I *would* risk it all!

ADELAIDE ANNE PROCTER

SHE WAS A PHANTOM OF DELIGHT

She was a phantom of delight
When first she gleamed upon my sight;
A lovely apparition, sent
To be a moment's ornament;
Her eyes as stars of twilight fair;
Like Twilight's, too, her dusky hair;
But all things else about her drawn
From May-time and the cheerful dawn;
A dancing shape, an image gay,
To haunt, to startle, and waylay.

I saw her upon nearer view,
A spirit, yet a woman too!
Her household motions light and free,
And steps of virgin-liberty;
A countenance in which did meet
Sweet records, promises as sweet;
A creature not too bright or good
For human nature's daily food,
For transient sorrows, simple wiles,
Praise, blame, love, kisses, tears, and smiles.

And now I see with eye serene
The very pulse of the machine;
A being breathing thoughtful breath,
A traveller between life and death:
The reason firm, the temperate will,
Endurance, foresight, strength, and skill;
A perfect woman, nobly planned
To warn, to comfort, and command;
And yet a spirit still, and bright
With something of an angel-light.

WILLIAM WORDSWORTH

FIRST LOVE

I ne'er was struck before that hour
  With love so sudden and so sweet,
Her face it bloomed like a sweet flower
  And stole my heart away complete.
My face turned pale as deadly pale,
  My legs refused to walk away,
And when she looked, what could I ail?
  My life and all seemed turned to clay.

And then my blood rushed to my face
  And took my eyesight quite away,
The trees and bushes round the place
  Seemed midnight at noonday.
I could not see a single thing,
  Words from my eyes did start—
They spoke as chords do from the string,
  And blood burnt round my heart.

Are flowers the winter's choice?
  Is love's bed always snow?
She seemed to hear my silent voice,
  Not love's appeals to know.
I never saw so sweet a face
  As that I stood before.
My heart has left its dwelling-place
  And can return no more.

JOHN CLARE

SONNET

I wish I could remember that first day,
　　First hour, first moment of your meeting me,
　　If bright or dim the season, it might be
Summer or winter for aught I can say;
So unrecorded did it slip away,
　　So blind was I to see and to foresee,
　　So dull to mark the budding of my tree
That would not blossom yet for many a May.
If only I could recollect it, such
　　A day of days! I let it come and go
　　As traceless as a thaw of bygone snow;
It seemed to mean so little, meant so much;
If only now I could recall that touch,
　　First touch of hand in hand—Did one but know!

CHRISTINA ROSSETTI

BELIEVE ME, IF ALL THOSE
ENDEARING YOUNG CHARMS

Believe me, if all those endearing young charms,
  Which I gaze on so fondly to-day,
Were to change by to-morrow, and fleet in my arms,
  Like fairy-gifts fading away!
Thou wouldst still be adored, as this moment thou art,
  Let thy loveliness fade as it will,
And around the dear ruin each wish of my heart
Would entwine itself verdantly still.

It is not while beauty and youth are thine own,
  And thy cheeks unprofaned by a tear,
That the fervor and faith of a soul may be known,
  To which time will but make thee more dear!
O the heart that has truly loved never forgets,
  But as truly loves on to the close,
As the sunflower turns to her god when he sets
  The same look which she turned when he rose!

THOMAS MOORE

TO CELIA

*D*rink to me only with thine eyes,
　And I will pledge with mine;
Or leave a kiss but in the cup,
　And I'll not look for wine.
The thirst that from the soul doth rise
　Doth ask a drink divine;
But might I of Jove's nectar sup,
　I would not change for thine.

I sent thee, late, a rosy wreath,
　Not so much honoring thee,
As giving it a hope that there
　It could not withered be.
But thou thereon did'st only breathe,
　And sent'st it back to me;
Since when, it grows, and smells, I swear,
　Not of itself, but thee.

PHILOSTRATUS
Translated from the Greek by Ben Jonson

LOVE

$\int$ love you,
Not only for what you are,
But for what I am
When I am with you.

$\int$ love you,
Not only for what
You have made of yourself,
But for what
You are making of me.

$\int$ love you
For the part of me
That you bring out;
I love you
For putting your hand
Into my heaped-up heart
And passing over
All the foolish, weak things
That you can't help
Dimly seeing there,
And for drawing out
Into the light
All the beautiful belongings
That no one else had looked
Quite far enough to find.

I love you because you
Are helping me to make
Of the lumber of my life
Not a tavern
But a temple;
Out of the works
Of my every day
Not a reproach
But a song.

I love you
Because you have done
More than any creed
Could have done
To make me good,
And more than any fate
Could have done
To make me happy.

You have done it
Without a touch,
Without a word,
Without a sign.
You have done it
By being yourself.
Perhaps that is what
Being a friend means,
After all.

ROY CROFT

MY LUVE'S LIKE A RED,
RED ROSE

O my Luve's like a red, red rose
   That's newly sprung in June:
O my Luve's like the melodie
   That's sweetly played in tune.
As fair art thou, my bonnie lass,
   So deep in luve am I:
And I will luve thee still, my dear,
   Till a' the seas gang dry:

Till a' the seas gang dry, my Dear,
   And the rocks melt wi' the sun;
I will luve thee still, my dear,
   While the sands o' life shall run.
And fare thee weel, my only Luve!
   And fare thee weel awhile!
And I will come again, my Luve,
   Tho' it were ten thousand mile.

ROBERT BURNS

TO MARY

I sleep with thee, and wake with thee,
  And yet thou art not there;
I fill my arms with thoughts of thee,
  And press the common air.
Thy eyes are gazing upon mine,
  When thou art out of sight;
My lips are always touching thine,
  At morning, noon, and night.

I think and speak of other things
  To keep my mind at rest:
But still to thee my memory clings
  Like love in woman's breast.
I hide it from the world's wide eye,
  And think and speak contrary;
But soft the wind comes from the sky,
  And whispers tales of Mary.

The night wind whispers in my ear,
  The moon shines in my face;
A burden still of chilling fear
  I find in every place.
The breeze is whispering in the bush,
  And the dews fall from the tree,
All sighing on, and will not hush,
  Some pleasant tales of thee.

JOHN CLARE

FREEDOM AND LOVE

How delicious is the winning
Of a kiss at love's beginning,
When two mutual hearts are sighing
For the knot there's no untying!

Yet remember, 'midst our wooing,
Love has bliss, but Love has ruing;
Other smiles may make you fickle,
Tears for other charms may trickle.

Love he comes, and Love he tarries,
Just as fate or fancy carries;
Longest stays, when sorest chidden;
Laughs and flies, when press'd and bidden.

Bind the sea to slumber stilly,
Bind its odour to the lily,
Bind the aspen ne'er to quiver,
Then bind Love to last for ever.

Love's a fire that needs renewal
Of fresh beauty for its fuel:
Love's wing moults when caged and captured,
Only free, he soars enraptured.

Can you keep the bee from ranging
Or the ringdove's neck from changing?
No! nor fetter'd Love from dying
In the knot there's no untying.

THOMAS CAMPBELL

TO ———

*T*oo late I stayed—forgive the crime—
   Unheeded flew the hours:
How noiseless falls the foot of Time
   That only treads on flowers!

And who, with clear account, remarks
   The ebbings of his glass,
When all its sands are diamond sparks,
   That dazzle as they pass?

Ah! who to sober measurement
   Time's happy swiftness brings,
When birds of paradise have lent
   Their plumage to his wings?

Robert William Spencer

GO, LOVELY ROSE

Go, lovely rose!
Tell her that wastes her time and me,
That now she knows,
When I resemble her to thee,
How sweet and fair she seems to be.

Tell her that's young,
And shuns to have her graces spied,
That hadst thou sprung
In deserts, where no men abide,
Thou must have uncommended died.

Small is the worth
Of beauty from the light retired;
Bid her come forth,
Suffer herself to be desired,
And not blush so to be admired.

Then die, that she
The common fate of all things rare
May read in thee;
How small a part of time they share,
That are so wondrous, sweet, and fair.

Edmund Waller

THE FLOWER'S NAME

Here's the garden she walked across,
　　Arm in my arm, such a short while since:
Hark! now I push its wicket, the moss
　　Hinders the hinges, and makes them wince.
She must have reached this shrub ere she turned,
　　As back with that murmur the wicket swung;
For she laid the poor snail my chance foot spurned,
　　To feed and forget it the leaves among.

　Down this side of the gravel walk
　　She went while her robe's edge brushed the box;
And here she paused in her gracious talk
　　To point me a moth on the milk-white phlox.
Roses, ranged in valiant row,
　　I will never think that she passed you by!
She loves you, noble roses, I know;
　　But yonder see where the rock-plants lie!

This flower she stopped at, finger on lip,—
　　Stooped over, in doubt, as settling its claim;
Till she gave me, with pride to make no slip,
　　Its soft meandering Spanish name.
What a name! was it love or praise?
　　Speech half asleep, or song half awake?
I must learn Spanish one of these days,
　　Only for that slow sweet name's sake.

　Roses, if I live and do well,
　　I may bring her one of these days,
To fix you fast with as fine a spell,—
　　Fit you each with his Spanish phrase.
But do not detain me now, for she lingers
　　There, like sunshine over the ground;
And ever I see her soft white fingers
　　Searching after the bud she found.

Flower, you Spaniard! look that you grow not,—
   Stay as you are, and be loved forever.
Bud, if I kiss you, 't is that you blow not,—
   Mind! the shut pink mouth opens never!
For while thus it pouts, her fingers wrestle,
   Twinkling the audacious leaves between,
Till round they turn, and down they nestle:
   Is not the dear mark still to be seen?

Where I find her not, beauties vanish;
   Whither I follow her, beauties flee.
Is there no method to tell her in Spanish
   June's twice June since she breathed it with me?
Come, bud! show me the least of her traces.
   Treasure my lady's lightest footfall:
Ah! you may flout and turn up your faces,—
   Roses, you are not so fair after all!

ROBERT BROWNING

LOVE NOT ME FOR
COMELY GRACE

Love not me for comely grace,
For my pleasing eye or face,
Nor for any outward part,
No, nor for my constant heart;
   For those may fail or turn to ill,
     So thou and I shall sever;
Keep therefore a true woman's eye,
And love me still, but know not why.
   So hast thou the same reason still
     To dote upon me ever.

ANONYMOUS

SONG

Shall I love you like the wind, love,
    That is so fierce and strong,
That sweeps all barriers from its path
    And reeks not right or wrong?
The passion of the wind, love,
    Can never last for long.

Shall I love you like the fire, love,
    With furious heat and noise,
To waken in you all love's fears
    And little of love's joys?
The passion of the fire, love,
    Whate'er it finds; destroys.

I will love you like the stars, love,
    Set in the heavenly blue,
That only shine the brighter
    After weeping tears of dew;
Above the wind and fire, love,
    They love the ages through!

And when this life is o'er, love,
    With all its joys and jars,
We'll leave behind the wind and fire
    To wage their boisterous wars,—
Then we shall only be, love,
    The nearer to the stars!

R. W. RAYMOND

SONNET

Shall I compare thee to a Summer's day?
Thou art more lovely and more temperate:
Rough winds do shake the darling buds of May,
And Summer's lease hath all too short a date:
Sometime too hot the eye of heaven shines,
And often is his gold complexion dimmed;
And every fair from fair sometime declines,
By chance or nature's changing course untrimmed:
But thy eternal Summer shall not fade
Nor lose possession of that fair thou owest;
Nor shall Death brag thou wanderest in his shade,
When in eternal lines to time thou growest:
So long as men can breathe, or eyes can see,
So long lives this, and this gives life to thee.

WILLIAM SHAKESPEARE

THE LADY'S "YES"

"Yes," I answered you last night;
   "No," this morning, sir, I say.
Colors seen by candle-light
   Will not look the same by day.

When the viols played their best,
   Lamps above, and laughs below,
Love me sounded like a jest,
   Fit for *yes* or fit for *no*.

Call me false or call me free,
   Vow, whatever light may shine,
No man on your face shall see
   Any grief for change on mine.

Yet the sin is on us both;
   Time to dance is not to woo;
Wooing light makes fickle troth.
   Scorn of *me* recoils on *you*.

Learn to win a lady's faith
   Nobly, as the thing is high,
Bravely, as for life and death,
   With a loyal gravity.

Lead her from the festive boards,
   Point her to the starry skies,
Guard her, by your truthful words,
   Pure from courtship's flatteries.

By your truth she shall be true,
   Ever true, as wives of yore;
And her *yes,* once said to you,
   Shall be Yes forevermore.

ELIZABETH BARRETT BROWNING

FLY NOT YET

*F*ly not yet—'t is just the hour
When pleasure, like the midnight flower,
That scorns the eye of vulgar light,
Begins to bloom for sons of night,
    And maids who love the moon!
'T was but to bless these hours of shade
That beauty and the moon were made;
'T is then their soft attractions glowing
Set the tides and goblets flowing!
    O! stay,— O! stay,—
Joy so seldom weaves a chain
Like this to-night, that O! 't is pain
    To break its links so soon.

Fly not yet! the fount that played,
In times of old, through Ammon's shade,
Though icy cold by day it ran,
Yet still, like sounds of mirth, began
    To burn when night was near;
And thus should woman's heart and looks
At noon be cold as winter-brooks,
Nor kindle till the night, returning,
Brings their genial hour for burning.
    O! stay,— O! stay,—
When did morning ever break
And find such beaming eyes awake
    As those that sparkle here!

THOMAS MOORE

THE GOOD MORROW

Jwonder by my troth, what thou, and I
   Did, till we loved? were we not weaned till
      then,
But sucked on country pleasures, childishly?
   Or snorted we in the seven sleepers' den?
'Twas so; but this, all pleasures fancies be.
If ever any beauty I did see,
   Which I desired, and got, 'twas but a dream of
      thee.

And now good morrow to our waking souls,
   Which watch not one another out of fear;
For love, all love of other sights controls,
   And makes one little room, an every where.
Let sea-discoverers to new worlds have gone,
Let maps to others, worlds on worlds have
      shown,
Let us possess one world, each hath one, and is
   one.

My face in thine eye, thine in mine appears,
   And true plain hearts do in the faces rest,
Where can we find two better hemispheres
   Without sharp north, without declining west?
What ever dies, was not mixed equally;
If our two loves be one, or, thou and I
   Love so alike, that none do slacken, none can die.

JOHN DONNE

THE SHEPHERD TO HIS LOVE

Come, live with me, and be my love,
And we will all the pleasures prove
That valleys, groves, hills, and fields,
Woods or steepy mountains, yields.

There we will sit upon the rocks,
Seeing the shepherds feed their flocks
By shallow rivers, to whose falls
Melodious birds sing madrigals.

There will I make thee beds of roses
With a thousand fragrant posies;
A cap of flowers, and a kirtle,
Embroidered all with leaves of myrtle;

A gown made of the finest wool,
Which from our pretty lambs we pull;
Fair-lined slippers for the cold,
With buckles of the purest gold;

A belt of straw, and ivy buds,
With coral clasps and amber studs:
And if these pleasures may thee move,
Come, live with me, and be my love.

The shepherd swains shall dance and sing
For thy delight each May morning,
If these delights thy mind may move,
Then live with me, and be my love.

CHRISTOPHER MARLOWE

SONNETS FROM THE PORTUGUESE

Go from me. Yet I feel that I shall stand
Henceforward in thy shadow. Nevermore
Alone upon the threshold of my door
Of individual life, I shall command
The uses of my soul, nor lift my hand
Serenely in the sunshine as before,
Without the sense of that which I forbore, . . .
Thy touch upon the palm. The widest land
Doom takes to part us, leaves thy heart in mine
With pulses that beat double. What I do
And what I dream include thee, as the wine
Must taste of its own grapes. And when I sue
God for myself, He hears that name of thine,
And sees within my eyes the tears of two.

If thou must love me, let it be for naught
Except for love's sake only. Do not say
"I love her for her smile . . . her look . . . her way
Of speaking gently,—for a trick of thought
That falls in well with mine, and certes brought
A sense of pleasant ease on such a day."
For these things in themselves, beloved, may
Be changed, or change for thee,—and love so
     wrought,
May be unwrought so. Neither love me for
Thine own dear pity's wiping my cheeks dry,—
A creature might forget to weep, who bore
Thy comfort long, and lose thy love thereby.
But love me for love's sake, that evermore
Thou mayst love on, through love's eternity.

𝓗ow do I love thee? Let me count the ways.
I love thee to the depth and breadth and height
My soul can reach, when feeling out of sight
For the ends of Being and ideal Grace.
I love thee to the level of every day's
Most quiet need, by sun and candlelight.
I love thee freely, as men strive for Right;
I love thee purely, as they turn from Praise.
I love thee with the passion put to use
In my old griefs, and with my childhood's faith.
I love thee with a love I seemed to lose
With my lost saints,—I love thee with the breath,
Smiles, tears, of all my life!—and, if God choose,
I shall but love thee better after death.

ELIZABETH BARRETT BROWNING

TO ALTHEA FROM PRISON

When Love with unconfinéd wings
  Hovers within my gates,
And my divine Althea brings
  To whisper at the grates;
When I lie tangled in her hair
  And fettered to her eye,
The birds that wanton in the air
  Know no such liberty.

When flowing cups run swiftly round
  With no allaying Thames,
Our careless heads with roses crowned,
  Our hearts with loyal flames;
When thirsty grief in wine we steep,
  When healths and draughts go free,
Fishes that tipple in the deep
  Know no such liberty.

When, linnet-like confinéd, I
  With shriller throat shall sing
The sweetness, mercy, majesty
  And glories of my King;
When I shall voice aloud how good
  He is, how great should be,
Enlargéd winds, that curl the flood,
  Know no such liberty.

Stone walls do not a prison make,
  Nor iron bars a cage;
Minds innocent and quiet take
  That for an hermitage:
If I have freedom in my love,
  And in my soul am free,
Angels alone, that soar above,
  Enjoy such liberty.

RICHARD LOVELACE

TO MY DEAR AND LOVING HUSBAND

*J*f ever two were one, then surely we.
If ever man were lov'd by wife, then thee.
If ever wife was happy in a man,
Compare with me, ye women, if you can.
I prize thy love more than whole Mines of gold,
Or all the riches that the East doth hold.
My love is such that Rivers cannot quench,
Nor ought but love from thee give recompence.
Thy love is such I can no way repay;
The heavens reward thee manifold I pray.
Then while we live, in love lets so persever,
That when we live no more, we may live ever.

ANNE BRADSTREET

THE POET'S SONG TO HIS WIFE

*H*ow many summers, love,
   Have I been thine?
How many days, thou dove,
   Hast thou been mine?
Time, like the winged wind
   When 't bends the flowers,
Hath left no mark behind,
   To count the hours!

Some weight of thought, though loth,
   On thee he leaves;
Some lines of care round both
   Perhaps he weaves;
Some fears,—a soft regret
   For joys scarce known;
Sweet looks we half forget;—
   All else is flown!

Ah!—With what thankless heart
   I mourn and sing!
Look, where our children start,
   Like sudden Spring!
With tongues all sweet and low,
   Like a pleasant rhyme,
They tell how much I owe
   To thee and Time!

BARRY CORNWALL

GIVE ALL TO LOVE

Give all to love;
Obey thy heart;
Friends, kindred, days,
Estate, good-fame,
Plans, credit, and the Muse,—
Nothing refuse.

'Tis a brave master;
Let it have scope:
Follow it utterly,
Hope beyond hope:
High and more high
It dives into noon,
With wing unspent,
Untold intent;
But it is a god,
Knows its own path,
And the outlets of the sky.

It was not for the mean;
It requireth courage stout,
Souls above doubt,
Valor unbending;
It will reward,—
They shall return
More than they were,
And ever ascending.

Leave all for love;
Yet, hear me, yet,
One word more thy heart behoved,
One pulse more of firm endeavor,—
Keep thee today,
To-morrow, forever,
Free as an Arab
Of thy beloved.

Cling with life to the maid;
But when the surprise,
First vague shadow of surmise
Flits across her bosom young
Of a joy apart from thee,
Free be she, fancy-free;
Nor thou detain her vesture's hem,
Nor the palest rose she flung
From her summer diadem.

RALPH WALDO EMERSON

LOVE ME LITTLE, LOVE ME LONG

Originally Printed in 1569

*L*ove me little, love me long!
Is the burden of my song:
Love that is too hot and strong
    Burneth soon to waste.
Still I would not have thee cold,—
Not too backward, nor too bold;
Love that lasteth till 't is old
    Fadeth not in haste.
Love me little, love me long!
Is the burden of my song.

If thou lovest me too much,
'T will not prove as true a touch;
Love me little more than such,—
    For I fear the end.
I'm with little well content,
And a little from thee sent
Is enough, with true intent
    To be steadfast, friend.

Say thou lovest me, while thou live
I to thee my love will give,
Never dreaming to deceive
    While that life endures;
Nay, and after death, in sooth,
I to thee will keep my truth,
As now when in my May of youth:
    This my love assures.

Constant love is moderate ever,
And it will through life persever;
Give me that with true endeavòr,—
    I will it restore.
A suit of durance let it be,
For all weathers,—that for me,—
For the land or for the sęa:
    Lasting evermore.

Winter's cold or summer's heat,
Autumn's tempests on it beat;
It can never know defeat,
    Never can rebel:
Such the love that I would gain,
Such the love, I tell thee plain,
Thou must give, or woo in vain:
    So to thee—farewell!

ANONYMOUS

LOVE'S PHILOSOPHY

The fountains mingle with the river,
   And the rivers with the ocean;
The winds of heaven mix forever,
   With a sweet emotion;
Nothing in the world is single;
   All things by a law divine
In one another's being mingle:—
   Why not I with thine?

See! the mountains kiss high heaven,
   And the waves clasp one another;
No sister flower would be forgiven
   If it disdained its brother;
And the sunlight clasps the earth,
   And the moonbeams kiss the sea:—
What are all these kissings worth,
   If thou kiss not me?

PERCY BYSSHE SHELLEY

TO A MAID DEMURE

Often when the night is come,
With its quiet group at home,
While they broider, knit, or sew,
Read, or chat in voices low,
Suddenly you lift your eyes
With an earnest look, and wise;
But I cannot read their lore,
Tell me less, or tell me more.

Like a picture in a book,
Pure and peaceful is your look,
Quietly you walk your ways;
Steadfast duty fills the days.
Neither tears nor fierce delights,
Feverish days nor tossing nights,
Any troublous dreams confess,—
Tell me more, or tell me less.

Swift the weeks are on the wing;
Years are brief, and love a thing
Blooming, fading, like a flower;
Wake and seize the little hour.
Give me welcome, or farewell;
Quick! I wait! And who can tell
What to-morrow may befall,—
Love me more, or not at all.

EDWARD ROWLAND SILL

}53{

GO WHERE GLORY
WAITS THEE!

Go where glory waits thee;
But, while Fame elates thee,
  O still remember me!
When the praise thou meetest
To thine ear is sweetest,
  O then remember me!
Other arms may press thee,
Dearer friends caress thee—
All the joys that bless thee
  Sweeter far may be;
But when friends are nearest,
And when joys are dearest,
  O then remember me!

When, at eve, thou rovest
By the star thou lovest,
   O then remember me!
Think when home returning,
Bright we've seen it burning,
   O, thus remember me!
Oft as summer closes,
When thine eye reposes
On its lingering roses,
   Once so loved by thee,
Think of her who wove them,
Her who made thee love them;
   O then remember me!

When, around thee dying,
Autumn leaves are lying,
   O then remember me!
And, at night, when gazing
On the gay hearth blazing,
   O, still remember me!
Then should music, stealing
All the soul of feeling,
To thy heart appealing,
   Draw one tear from thee—
Then let memory bring thee
Strains I used to sing thee;
   O then remember me!

THOMAS MOORE

NON SUM QUALIS ERAM BONAE SUB REGNO CYNARAE

Last night, ah, yesternight, betwixt her lips and mine
There fell thy shadow, Cynara! Thy breath was shed
Upon my soul between the kisses and the wine;
And I was desolate and sick of an old passion—
Yea, I was desolate and bowed my head.
I have been faithful to thee, Cynara!—In my fashion.

All night upon mine heart I felt her warm heart beat,
Night-long within mine arms in love and sleep she lay;
Surely the kisses of her bought red mouth were sweet;
But I was desolate and sick of an old passion,
When I woke and found the dawn was gray:
I have been faithful to thee, Cynara!—In my fashion.

I have forgot much, Cynara! Gone with the wind,
Flung roses, roses riotously with the throng,
Dancing, to put thy pale, lost lilies out of mind;
But I was desolate and sick of an old passion—
Yea, all the time, because the dance was long:
I have been faithful to thee, Cynara!—In my fashion.

I cried for madder music and for stronger wine,
But when the feast is finished and the lamps expire,
Then falls thy shadow, Cynara! The night is thine;
And I am desolate and sick of an old passion,
Yea, hungry for the lips of my desire:
I have been faithful to thee, Cynara!—In my fashion.

ERNEST DOWSON

AT THE CHURCH GATE

Although I enter not,
Yet round about the spot
    Ofttimes I hover;
And near the sacred gate,
With longing eyes I wait,
    Expectant of her.

The minster bell tolls out
Above the city's rout,
    And noise and humming;
They've hushed the minster bell;
The organ 'gins to swell;
    She's coming, coming!

My lady comes at last,
Timid and stepping fast,
    And hastening hither,
With modest eyes downcast;
She comes,—she's here, she's past!
    May Heaven go with her!

Kneel undisturbed, fair saint!
Pour out your praise or plaint
    Meekly and duly;
I will not enter there,
To sully your pure prayer
    With thoughts unruly.

But suffer me to pace
Round the forbidden place,
    Lingering a minute,
Like outcast spirits, who wait,
And see, through heaven's gate,
    Angels within it.

WILLIAM MAKEPEACE THACKERAY

SONG

Why so pale and wan, fond lover?
  Pr'y thee, why so pale?—
Will, when looking well can't move her,
  Looking ill prevail?
  Pr'y thee, why so pale?

Why so dull and mute, young sinner?
  Pr'y thee, why so mute?—
Will, when speaking well can't win her,
  Saying nothing do't?
  Pr'y thee, why so mute?

Quit, quit, for shame! this will not move,
  This cannot take her—
If of herself she will not love,
  Nothing can make her:
  The Devil take her!

JOHN SUCKLING

APRIL LOVE

We have walked in Love's land a little way,
  We have learnt his lesson a little while,
And shall we not part at the end of day,
    With a sigh, a smile?

A little while in the shine of the sun,
  We were twined together, joined lips forgot
How the shadows fall when the day is done,
    And when Love is not.

We have made no vows—there will none be broke,
  Our love was free as the wind on the hill,
There was no word said we need wish unspoke,
    We have wrought no ill.

So shall we not part at the end of day,
  Who have loved and lingered a little while,
Join lips for the last time, go our way,
    With a sigh, a smile.

ERNEST DOWSON

WE PARTED IN SILENCE

We parted in silence, we parted by night,
　On the banks of that lonely river;
Where the fragrant limes their boughs unite,
　We met—and we parted for ever!
The night-bird sung, and the stars above
　Told many a touching story,
Of friends long passed to the kingdom of love,
　Where the soul wears its mantle of glory.

We parted in silence—our cheeks were wet
　With the tears that were past controlling;
We vowed we would never—no, never forget,
　And those vows at the time were consoling;
But those lips that echoed the wounds of mine
　Are as cold as that lonely river;
And that eye, that beautiful spirit's shrine,
　Has shrouded its fires for ever.

And now on the midnight sky I look,
　And my heart grows full of weeping;
Each star is to me a sealed book,
　Some tale of that loved one keeping.
We parted in silence—we parted in tears,
　On the banks of that lonely river:
But the color and bloom of those by-gone years
　Shall hang o'er its waters for ever.

MRS. CRAWFORD

ADAM TO EVE

O fairest of creation, last and best
Of all God's works, creature in whom excelled
Whatever can to sight or thought be formed,
Holy, divine, good, amiable, or sweet!
How art thou lost, how on a sudden lost,
Defaced, deflowered, and now to death devote!
Rather, how hast thou yielded to transgress
The strict forbiddance, how to violate.
The sacred fruit forbidden! Some cursèd fraud
Of enemy hath beguiled thee, yet unknown,
And me with thee hath ruined, for with thee
Certain my resolution is to die.
How can I live without thee, how forego
Thy sweet converse, and love so dearly joined,
To live again in these wild woods forlorn?
Should God create another Eve, and I
Another rib afford, yet loss of thee
Would never from my heart; no, no, I feel
The link of nature draw me: flesh of flesh,
Bone of my bone thou art, and from thy state
Mine never shall be parted, bliss or woe.

. . . . .

However, I with thee have fixed my lot,
Certain to undergo like doom; if death
Consort with thee, death is to me as life;
So forcible within my heart I feel
The bond of nature draw me to my own,
My own in thee, for what thou art is mine;
Our state cannot be severed, we are one,
One flesh; to lose thee were to lose myself.

JOHN MILTON

ANNABEL LEE

It was many and many a year ago,
  In a kingdom by the sea,
That a maiden there lived whom you may know
  By the name of Annabel Lee;
And this maiden she lived with no other thought
  Than to love and be loved by me.

I was a child and she was a child,
  In this kingdom by the sea,
But we loved with a love that was more than love,
  I and my Annabel Lee;
With a love that the wingèd seraphs of heaven
  Coveted her and me.

And this was the reason that, long ago,
  In this kingdom by the sea,
A wind blew out of a cloud, chilling
  My beautiful Annabel Lee;

So that her highborn kinsman came
    And bore her away from me,
To shut her up in a sepulcher
    In this kingdom by the sea.

The angels, not half so happy in heaven,
    Went envying her and me;
Yes! that was the reason (as all men know,
    In this kingdom by the sea)
That the wind came out of the cloud by night,
    Chilling and killing my Annabel Lee.

But our love it was stronger by far than the love
    Of those who were older than we,
    Of many far wiser than we;
And neither the angels in heaven above,
    Nor the demons down under the sea,
Can ever dissever my soul from the soul
    Of the beautiful Annabel Lee:

For the moon never beams, without bringing me dreams
    Of the beautiful Annabel Lee;
And the stars never rise, but I feel the bright eyes
    Of the beautiful Annabel Lee;
And so, all the night-tide, I lie down by the side
Of my darling—my darling—my life and my bride,
    In her sepulcher there by the sea,
    In her tomb by the sounding sea.

EDGAR ALLAN POE

LOVE WHAT IT IS

*L*ove is a circle that
doth restless move
In the same sweet
eternity of love.

ROBERT HERRICK